COUNTRIES OF THE WORLD

UNITED STATES

ABDO
Publishing Company

UNITED STATES

by Robert Grayson

Content Consultant
Katrina Lacher, PhD, Assistant Professor
Department of History and Geography, University of Central Oklahoma

CREDITS

Published by ABDO Publishing Company, PO Box 398166, Minneapolis, MN 55439.
Copyright © 2013 by Abdo Consulting Group, Inc. International copyrights reserved
in all countries. No part of this book may be reproduced in any form without written
permission from the publisher. The Essential Library™ is a trademark and logo of ABDO
Publishing Company.

Printed in the United States of America,
North Mankato, Minnesota
112012
012013

Editor: Rebecca Felix
Series Designer: Emily Love

About the Author: Robert Grayson is an award-winning former daily newspaper
reporter and the author of books for young adults. Throughout his journalism career,
Grayson has written stories on historic events, sports figures, arts & entertainment,
business, and pets. He has written books about the Industrial Revolution, the California
Gold Rush, animals in the military, and animal performers as well as the environment, law
enforcement, and professional sports.

Cataloging-in-Publication Data

Grayson, Robert.
 United States / Robert Grayson.
   p. cm. -- (Countries of the world)
Includes bibliographical references and index.
ISBN 978-1-61783-640-4
1. United States--Juvenile literature.   I. Title.
973--dc22

2012946085

Cover: The US Capitol building in Washington DC

TABLE OF CONTENTS

CHAPTER 1

A VISIT TO THE UNITED STATES

You carefully map out your visit to the United States like a journey through time. The United States celebrates its extraordinary past by preserving national landmarks and historic sites across its vast countryside. These time capsules allow you to reconstruct the story of a nation built on the principles of freedom and democracy.

You start your trip along the Eastern Seaboard, the site of the original 13 American colonies. The struggle for independence is proudly documented throughout this region. As you stand in the middle of Minute Man National Historic Park in eastern Massachusetts, you feel the resolve of the patriots who fought in the American Revolution. The park encompasses the battlefields of Lexington and Concord, where the first military encounters between the colonists and the British in the War of Independence (1775–1782) took place on April 19, 1775.

Throughout the United States, sites such as Gettysburg preserve and honor the nation's history.

Traveling approximately 450 miles (724 km) southwest of Concord, you reach Gettysburg, Pennsylvania, where a different war is memorialized. Somber memories of the American Civil War (1861–1865) still linger over Gettysburg National Military Park, a former battlefield where President Abraham Lincoln gave his famous Gettysburg Address.

A victory here by Northern troops during a key battle in July 1863 became a major turning point in the bitterly divisive war between the North and the South.

Next you travel along the mid-Atlantic Coast to visit the nation's capital in Washington DC, which is home to many significant historical sites. One site in particular is a spectacular symbol of democracy and architectural grandeur—the US Capitol. The House of Representatives and the Senate have met and conducted business in the gleaming white Capitol for more than 200 years.

CAPITAL CITY

Founded in 1791, Washington DC was specifically formed to be a government seat and the nation's capital. It is not a part of any state but is instead considered an independent district. Washington DC holds much to see, including the National Mall, a 146-acre (59 ha), tree-lined park with a reflecting pool that serves as a centerpiece for much of the Capital District in the city. Other sights on the mall include the Washington Monument, the Vietnam Veterans Memorial, and the Constitution Gardens. The National Mall sits between the Capitol and the Lincoln Memorial. The White House, the official residence of the nation's president, is also nearby. Construction on the White House began in 1792 and was completed in 1800. Every US president, except for the first one, George Washington, who served from 1789 to 1797, has lived in the White House.

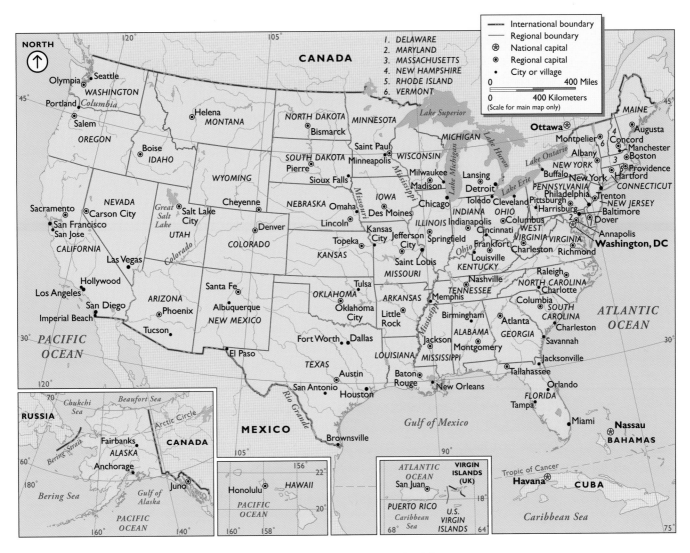

NORTH ↑

CANADA

| International boundary |
| Regional boundary |
| ⊛ National capital |
| ◉ Regional capital |
| • City or village |

1. DELAWARE
2. MARYLAND
3. MASSACHUSETTS
4. NEW HAMPSHIRE
5. RHODE ISLAND
6. VERMONT

0 _____ 400 Miles
0 _____ 400 Kilometers
(Scale for main map only)

Olympia • Seattle
WASHINGTON
Portland • Columbia
Salem •
OREGON
Helena •
MONTANA
NORTH DAKOTA
Bismarck •
MINNESOTA
Lake Superior
MICHIGAN
Ottawa ⊛
MAINE
Montpelier • Augusta
Concord • Manchester
Boston •
NEW YORK
Albany •
Providence
Hartford
CONNECTICUT

Boise •
IDAHO
SOUTH DAKOTA
Pierre •
Saint Paul
Minneapolis
WISCONSIN
Madison •
Milwaukee
Lansing •
Detroit •
NEW YORK
Buffalo • New York
PENNSYLVANIA
Philadelphia
NEW JERSEY
Trenton

WYOMING
Sioux Falls
Mississippi
IOWA
Chicago •
Toledo • Cleveland • Pittsburgh
Harrisburg
Baltimore
Dover

Sacramento •
NEVADA
Carson City •
Great Salt Lake
Salt Lake City •
UTAH
Cheyenne •
NEBRASKA
Omaha •
Des Moines •
INDIANA
OHIO
Columbus •
Cincinnati •
WEST
VIRGINIA
VIRGINIA
Annapolis
Washington, DC

San Francisco •
San Jose •
CALIFORNIA
Denver •
COLORADO
Lincoln •
Kansas City
Topeka •
KANSAS
Jefferson City
Springfield •
ILLINOIS Indianapolis •
Frankfort •
KENTUCKY
Louisville •
Charleston •
Richmond •

Las Vegas •
Colorado
Saint Louis •
MISSOURI
Ohio

Hollywood •
Los Angeles •
Santa Fe •
ARIZONA
Tulsa •
OKLAHOMA
Nashville •
TENNESSEE
Memphis •
Raleigh •
NORTH CAROLINA
Charlotte •

San Diego •
Imperial Beach •
Phoenix •
Albuquerque •
NEW MEXICO
Oklahoma City •
Little Rock •
ARKANSAS
Birmingham •
Columbia •
SOUTH CAROLINA
Charleston •

Tucson •
ALABAMA
GEORGIA
Atlanta •
Savannah •

PACIFIC OCEAN

El Paso •
TEXAS
Fort Worth • Dallas •
Jackson •
MISSISSIPPI
Montgomery •
ATLANTIC OCEAN

Austin •
San Antonio •
Houston •
LOUISIANA
Baton Rouge •
New Orleans •
Jacksonville •
Tallahassee •
Orlando •
FLORIDA
Tampa •

Rio Grande
Brownsville •
Gulf of Mexico
Miami •
Nassau •
BAHAMAS

MEXICO

RUSSIA
Chukchi Sea
Beaufort Sea
Arctic Circle
CANADA
Fairbanks •
ALASKA
Anchorage •
Bering Strait
Bering Sea
Gulf of Alaska
Juno •
PACIFIC OCEAN

HAWAII
Honolulu •
PACIFIC OCEAN

ATLANTIC OCEAN
San Juan •
PUERTO RICO
Caribbean Sea
VIRGIN ISLANDS (UK)
U.S. VIRGIN ISLANDS

Tropic of Cancer
Havana •
CUBA
Caribbean Sea

Political Boundaries of the United States

Farther south along the Atlantic Coast, on the Outer Banks of North Carolina, you come upon the place where the Wright Brothers first succeeded in getting an airplane off the ground. A testament to the nation's spirit of inventiveness, the memory of that December 1903 flight forever clings to the wind and sand here.

THIRST FOR ADVENTURE

Next you recapture the American thirst for adventure by following the trail of explorers Meriwether Lewis and William Clark. The fearless pair traveled by boat, on horseback, and on foot during their expedition, but you take more modern transportation, such as a car, to retrace their steps. You track their every move along approximately 3,700 miles (6,000 km) of their route, commemorated by the Lewis and Clark National Historic Trail that meanders through 11 states. You go from Illinois in the Midwest into the heart of what was the Missouri Territory. You continue west to the rolling hills of Nebraska, onto the grassy expanse of the Great Plains, and to the dense, green Pacific Northwest. You look out across the landscape, imagining what it was like for Lewis and Clark to explore this massive, uncharted terrain for the first time.

The landscape in the United States is varied and unique. Perhaps you long to scale a mountain range. You find the soaring, rugged Rocky

Lewis and Clark's exploration of the diverse US wilderness took them across many landscapes, including the towering Rocky Mountains.

Mountains in the West and the more modest Appalachian Mountains running north to south in the East. You bask in the immense wilderness and lush, grass-covered prairies in the Badlands of southwestern South Dakota. You stand awestruck as water splashes off the granite rock formations at the foot of the natural waterfalls in Yosemite National Park in California. You grab a pair of binoculars and spend frigid days watching fascinating wildlife, including caribou and otters, going about their daily routine in the natural habitat along the snowy Alaska Peninsula. You swelter in the heat of the West Coast's Mojave Desert, the hottest desert in North America, and then head east to the sandy beaches of Florida's west coast, where you sit beneath palm trees and swim in the Gulf of Mexico.

A DIVERSE NATION

When you visit the United States, you may just find someplace that makes you feel right at home. This is because the landscape and people in the United States mirror the rest of the world. People have immigrated to the United States from across the globe. These people brought their customs and traditions and wove them into a patchwork to create a multicultural country.

Numerous ethnic neighborhoods exist in the United States, especially in major cities. In Greektown in Chicago's West Loop, you can

The diversity of US neighborhoods creates a unique tapestry of people and cultures.

NEW YORK, NEW YORK

Of all the urban areas in the United States, New York City attracts the most tourists every year. Approximately 50 million people visit the city each year. That many people, added to the city's 8 million permanent residents, can make the city's 305 square miles (790 sq km) feel rather crowded at times. Considered the cultural capital of the world by many, New York City boasts an array of sights: Central Park, Times Square, Lincoln Center, the Statue of Liberty, Broadway, Rockefeller Center, the Empire State Building, the Metropolitan Museum of Art, the Bronx Zoo, and the New York Stock Exchange, to name just a few.

hear immigrants tell their stories at the National Hellenic Museum and then enjoy a gyro, which is meat wrapped in flatbread, in a nearby shop. You can stand under the iconic stone Gateway Arch in San Francisco's Chinatown, the oldest Chinatown of several in North America. In New York City's Little Italy, you can attend the 11-day Feast of San Gennaro, which celebrates Italian cuisine and culture each September on Mulberry Street.

These diverse neighborhoods, and others like them throughout the United States, are rich in authentic cultural experiences, providing native cuisine, groceries, crafts, folk art, and textiles of many cultures. Diverse ethnicities and cultures allow Americans to enjoy their individual culture and experience other cultures across the nation.

SNAPSHOT

Official name: United States of America

Form of government: Constitution-based federal republic; strong democratic tradition

Title of leader: president

Currency: dollar

Population (July 2012 est.): 313,847,465
World rank: 3

Size: 3,794,100 square miles (9,826,675 sq km)
World rank: 3 (Note: Includes only the 50 states and the District of Columbia)

Language: English, 82.1 percent; Spanish, 10.7 percent; other Indo-European, 3.8 percent; Asian and Pacific island, 2.7 percent; other, 0.7 percent

Official religion (if any): none

Per capita GDP (2011, US dollars): $49,000
World rank: 11

CHAPTER 2

GEOGRAPHY: FROM THE MOUNTAINS TO THE PRAIRIES

The world's third-largest country by size, behind Russia and China, the United States is a geographic marvel.[1] It offers a blend of eastern coastal wetlands; a gentle, hilly eastern coastal plain; central lowlands of rolling terrain; marshes and bayous in the deep South; open spaces in the Great Plains;

GRAND CANYON

Reaching a depth of nearly 6,000 feet (1,829 m), the Grand Canyon in northern Arizona is an amazing sight. Carved out by the Colorado River at least 17 million years ago, the canyon is one of the Seven Natural Wonders of the World. It is 18 miles (29 km) wide and 277 miles (446 km) long and showcases stunning rock formations.

The Grand Canyon represents just a fraction of the varied geography in the United States, which includes deserts, coasts, forests, and plains.

deserts in the Southwest; and rocky plateaus and deep canyons in the mountains out West. The country is also blessed with many vital natural waterways. Large rivers, including the Mississippi, the Colorado, the Ohio, the Columbia, and the Missouri are breathtaking to behold and important to the nation for transportation and shipping.

Nestled in the middle of North America, the United States borders Mexico to the south and Canada to the north. The states called the "Lower 48," which include all but Alaska and Hawaii, are flanked by the Atlantic Ocean on the east and the Pacific Ocean on the west. Natural harbors created by the Atlantic and Pacific shorelines propelled the development of the nation's largest cities on both coasts. These include Boston, Massachusetts, and New York City on the East Coast, and San Francisco, California, and Seattle, Washington, on the West Coast. The Gulf of Mexico runs along the coast of five southern states: Texas, Louisiana, Mississippi, Alabama, and Florida.

The Mojave Desert lies in parts of four Western states: Arizona, California, Nevada, and Utah.

DISTINCTIVE REGIONS

The United States comprises several regions, each with specific characteristics. The Northeast is the oldest established region in the nation. It includes the nation's most populous city, New York City. It also holds the country's smallest state, Rhode Island, which is 37 miles (60 km) wide and 48 miles (77 km) long. The nation's capital, Washington DC, is also part of this region. The area hugs the Atlantic coastline on the east side, which

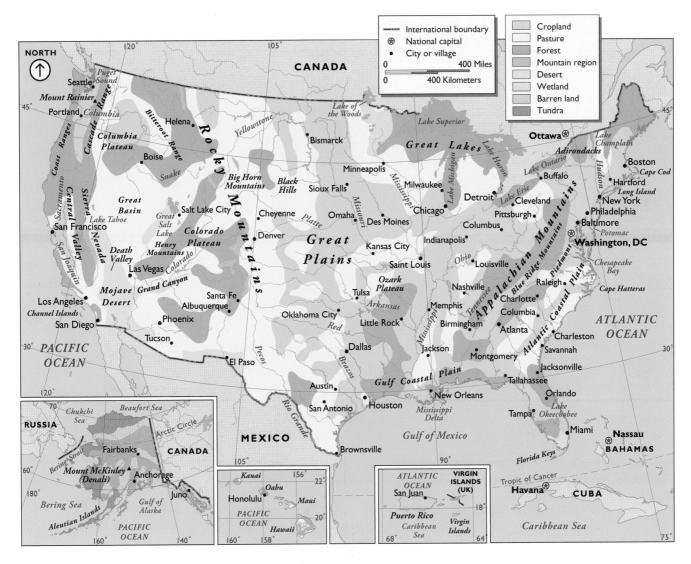

Map legend:

	International boundary
⊛	National capital
•	City or village

Scale: 0 — 400 Miles / 0 — 400 Kilometers

	Cropland
	Pasture
	Forest
	Mountain region
	Desert
	Wetland
	Barren land
	Tundra

Main map labels:

NORTH ↑

CANADA

Seattle • Puget Sound
Mount Rainier ▲
Portland • Columbia
Coast Ranges
Cascade Range
Columbia Plateau
Helena
Bitterroot Range
Boise
Snake
Great Basin
Sierra Nevada
Central Valley
Sacramento
San Francisco • Lake Tahoe
Death Valley
San Joaquin
Los Angeles
Channel Islands
San Diego
Mojave Desert
Grand Canyon
Las Vegas
Henry Mountains
Colorado Plateau
Great Salt Lake
Salt Lake City
Colorado
Phoenix
Tucson
El Paso
Santa Fe
Albuquerque
Rocky Mountains
Big Horn Mountains
Black Hills
Cheyenne
Denver
Yellowstone
Bismarck
Minneapolis
Sioux Falls
Missouri
Platte
Great Plains
Omaha
Des Moines
Kansas City
Saint Louis
Oklahoma City
Red
Dallas
Pecos
Brazos
Austin
San Antonio
Rio Grande
Brownsville
Houston
New Orleans
Mississippi Delta
Gulf Coastal Plain
Gulf of Mexico
Lake of the Woods
Lake Superior
Great Lakes
Lake Michigan
Lake Huron
Milwaukee
Chicago
Detroit
Lake Erie
Cleveland
Pittsburgh
Columbus
Indianapolis
Louisville
Ohio
Nashville
Memphis
Tulsa
Ozark Plateau
Arkansas
Little Rock
Birmingham
Jackson
Montgomery
Atlanta
Mississippi
Tennessee
Appalachian Mountains
Blue Ridge Mountains
Piedmont
Charlotte
Columbia
Charleston
Savannah
Jacksonville
Tallahassee
Orlando
Lake Okeechobee
Tampa
Miami
Florida Keys
Ottawa ⊛
Lake Ontario
Buffalo
Adirondacks
Lake Champlain
Hudson
Boston
Cape Cod
Hartford
Long Island
New York
Philadelphia
Baltimore
Washington, DC ⊛
Potomac
Chesapeake Bay
Atlantic Coastal Plain
Raleigh
Cape Hatteras
ATLANTIC OCEAN
PACIFIC OCEAN
Nassau ⊛
BAHAMAS
Havana ⊛
CUBA
Caribbean Sea
MEXICO
120° 105° 90° 75°
45° 45°
30° 30°
Tropic of Cancer

Alaska inset:
RUSSIA
Chukchi Sea
Beaufort Sea
Bering Strait
Fairbanks
Arctic Circle
CANADA
Mount McKinley (Denali) ▲
Anchorage
Juno
Gulf of Alaska
Bering Sea
Aleutian Islands
PACIFIC OCEAN
70° 60°
180° 160° 140°

Hawaii inset:
Kauai
Oahu
Honolulu
Maui
PACIFIC OCEAN
Hawaii
156° 158° 160°
22° 20°

Puerto Rico / Virgin Islands inset:
ATLANTIC OCEAN
VIRGIN ISLANDS (UK)
San Juan
Puerto Rico
Caribbean Sea
Virgin Islands
68° 64°
18°

Geography of the United States

begins with jagged cliffs at its northernmost point in Maine, and turns into sandy beach as it makes its way south. The Northeast also encompasses some islands, including Nantucket in Massachusetts, Block Island in Rhode Island, and Manhattan in New York.

Much of the flatlands in the Northeast, used for farming during colonial days, have been developed into thriving urban areas with large, concentrated populations and major business and entertainment meccas. Moving inland, there are numerous mountain ranges, including the Appalachians, which are considered the dividing line between the Atlantic coastal states and the Midwest.

The Midwest is in the central part of the nation and runs from the Appalachian Mountains in the east to the Rocky Mountains in the west. The Midwest is often called the heartland of the nation. The Central Lowlands in the Midwest, which lie to the west of the Appalachian Mountains, are mostly flatland with some gentle, rolling hills. Ice Age glaciers covered the Midwest thousands of years ago. When they receded, a multitude of lakes were formed, including the Great Lakes in the north. South of the Great Lakes, the massive moving sheets of ice left behind rich, fertile soil on the land that eventually became the states of Illinois, Indiana, Iowa, Minnesota, Missouri, Nebraska, Ohio, and Wisconsin.

A region in the Midwest with very few trees, known as the Great Plains, stretches southward from the Canadian border and west to the

The coast of Maine borders the Atlantic Ocean in the Northeast.

Several southern states, including Florida, have sandy beaches and warm temperatures year-round.

Rocky Mountains. Its grassy fields once fed large herds of American bison and helped feed the growing nation with acres of wheat farms. The heartland still provides much of the country's food. The Midwest also has many big cities, the largest of which is Chicago, Illinois. Other large Midwestern cities include Detroit, Michigan; Indianapolis, Indiana; Minneapolis, Minnesota; Saint Louis, Missouri; and Milwaukee, Wisconsin.

The southern United States is very geographically diverse. In the Southeast, the state of Georgia is in a mountainous region. Subtropical forestland characterizes much of Florida. Marshes abound in Louisiana. Rich farmland and sandy beaches also make up much of this region. The Southwest has deserts, mountains, plateaus, mesas, buttes, and flatlands. Although there are sprawling cities in the Southwest, such as Phoenix, Arizona, and Houston and Dallas in Texas, the region is a combination of urban areas and less-populated open spaces.

The West extends from the Rocky Mountains west to the Pacific Ocean. The scenery alternates from basins to mountain ranges and has many dry areas, including desert territory such as the famous Death Valley in California. Both volcanic and nonvolcanic mountains make up the

YELLOWSTONE IN THE ROCKY MOUNTAINS

The United States has preserved much of its natural parkland. Yellowstone, the world's oldest national park, is located in the Rocky Mountains in northwest Wyoming. Its 2.2 million acres (890,000 ha) are home to the internationally famous geyser Old Faithful, a hot spring that erupts periodically. An eruption from Old Faithful shoots water upwards of 145 feet (44 m) in the air. The fabled geyser is one of many within the park. Yellowstone has the largest concentration of active geysers anywhere in the world.

Cascade Mountain range, which runs through northern California and the states of Oregon and Washington into Canada. The highest peak in the Cascades is Washington's Mount Rainier. It is considered one of the world's most dangerous volcanoes, but it has not come close to erupting since the mid-nineteenth century.

Other mountain ranges in the West include the Rockies, the Pacific Coast Ranges, and the Sierra Nevada. A number of major cities are also out West, including Seattle, Washington; Portland, Oregon; and San Francisco and Los Angeles in California.

The two states outside the 48 contiguous states are Alaska and Hawaii. Alaska is in the northwest of the North American continent, bordering Canada. Hawaii

HAWAIIAN PILGRIMAGE

Hawaii was the fiftieth US state to be incorporated and is a popular travel destination for visitors to the United States. Hawaii is made up of a string of islands in the Pacific Ocean. In addition to a lush terrain of mountains and beaches, one of the state's biggest attractions is Pearl Harbor, the site of Japan's surprise attack on the United States on December 7, 1941. The attack brought the United States into World War II (1939–1945), killed approximately 2,400 people, and destroyed 21 battleships. Perhaps the most significant remembrance of that dark day is the USS *Arizona* Memorial, which sits atop the sunken battleship of the same name.[2]

Mount Rainier, in the Cascade Mountains of the Pacific Northwest, is surrounded by lush green forest.

is in the Pacific Ocean approximately 2,400 miles (3,862 km) west of southwest California.

The United States also has other regions that are not states. These include the US Virgin Islands, the Territory of American Samoa, the Territory of Guam, Kingman Reef, and the Commonwealth of Puerto Rico.

CLIMATE

Climate in the United States is as varied as its geography. Rainfall is common in the Pacific Northwest. The Great Lakes region gets heavy snow in the winter. The Great Plains is semiarid, while the deep South and much of California is subtropical. Hawaii and parts of Florida are tropical, and the Southwest is generally hot. Most parts of the United States experience each of the four seasons, but to differing degrees, depending on location. Regions in the far North, closer to Canada, are much colder than southern ones near the Gulf of Mexico and Mexico. The Midwest has harsh winters mixed in with its four seasons, as does New England in the Northeast. However, cold snaps can occur in the South and heat waves in the North. Extended dry spells in the East, Midwest, and West can cause damaging wildfires.

Temperatures in northern Alaska can dip to -80 degrees Fahrenheit (-62°C).

The East Coast is subject to damage from nor'easters, storms that can bring high winds and, depending on the season, heavy snow

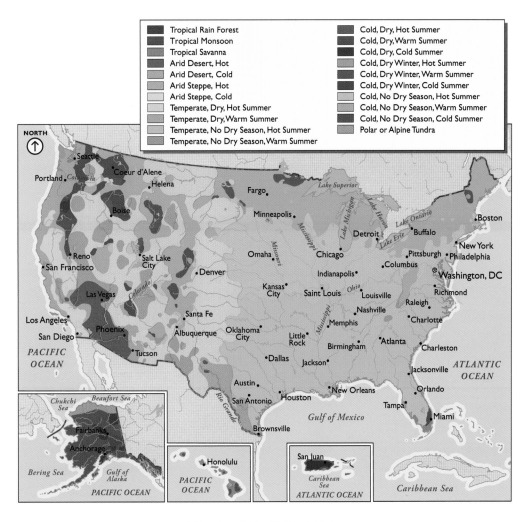

Legend:

- Tropical Rain Forest
- Tropical Monsoon
- Tropical Savanna
- Arid Desert, Hot
- Arid Desert, Cold
- Arid Steppe, Hot
- Arid Steppe, Cold
- Temperate, Dry, Hot Summer
- Temperate, Dry, Warm Summer
- Temperate, No Dry Season, Hot Summer
- Temperate, No Dry Season, Warm Summer
- Cold, Dry, Hot Summer
- Cold, Dry, Warm Summer
- Cold, Dry, Cold Summer
- Cold, Dry Winter, Hot Summer
- Cold, Dry Winter, Warm Summer
- Cold, Dry Winter, Cold Summer
- Cold, No Dry Season, Hot Summer
- Cold, No Dry Season, Warm Summer
- Cold, No Dry Season, Cold Summer
- Polar or Alpine Tundra

Climate of the United States

AVERAGE TEMPERATURE AND PRECIPITATION

Region (City)	Average January Temperature Minimum/Maximum	Average July Temperature Minimum/Maximum	Average Precipitation January/July
Northeast (New York City)	25/38°F (−3/3°C)	68/84°F (20/29°C)	3.3/4.2 inches (8.4/10.7 cm)
Southeast (Atlanta)	33/52°F (0/11°C)	70/89°F (21/31°C)	4.7/5.3 inches (11.9/13.5 cm)
Midwest (Chicago)	13/29°F (−10/−1°C)	63/84°F (17/28°C)	1.7/3.6 inches (4.3/9.1 cm)
Rocky Mountain Region (Denver)	16/43°F (−8/6°C)	59/88°F (15/31°C)	0.5/1.9 inches (1.3/4.8 cm)
Southwest (Phoenix)	41/61°F (5/18°C)	80/105°F (26/40°C)	0.8/0.8 inches (2.0/2.0 cm)
West Coast (Los Angeles)	42/67°F (5/20°C)	61/88°F (14/27°C)	3.4/0.0 inches (8.6/0.0 cm)
Pacific Northwest (Seattle)	36/45°F (2/7°C)	56/74°F (13/23°C)	5.1/0.7 inches (13.0/1.8 cm)[3]

or drenching rains. Tornadoes wreak havoc during spring and summer in the Great Plains and throughout the Midwest. Depending on where they touch down, these twisters can cause extensive loss of life and massive destruction.

The Atlantic Coast and the Gulf Coast are prime targets of hurricanes from June to November. Hurricanes are also a threat to the islands of Hawaii in the Pacific Ocean. With the large number of rivers and lakes in the United States, any storm that brings heavy, prolonged rainfall can also lead to flooding that puts nearby residential and business areas at risk.

CHAPTER 3
ANIMALS AND NATURE: WHERE EAGLES SOAR

In 1782, the nation's founders chose the bald eagle to symbolize the United States, reflecting their vision for the nation. The bald eagle is powerful and soars high and free. This magnificent bird of prey lives everywhere in the continental United States. It has even nested in busy urban neighborhoods, including Harlem in New York City.

A male and female pair will continue adding to a nest they built for years, making it bigger and bigger. In fact, one bald eagle nest found in Florida was so big it weighed more than two short tons (1.8 metric tons)! The giant nest was nine feet (2.7 m) wide and 20 feet (6 m) deep.[1]

Bald eagles build big nests because they are large birds. The length of their bodies can range from 29 to 42 inches (74 to 107 cm). Male bald

The bald eagle symbolizes the freedom and strength the United States strives to uphold.

eagles are lighter than females, weighing anywhere between six and nine pounds (2.7 and 4 kg). Females can be up to 14 pounds (6 kg). A bald eagle's wingspan is also large: it can be up to eight feet (2.4 m) wide.

A wide wingspan helps bald eagles soar. When they do flap their wings, they can reach speeds up to 44 miles per hour (69 km/h). When diving for food, however, this speed can accelerate to 200 miles per hour (322 km/h). Sharp eyesight allows the bald eagle to see prey up to one mile (1.6 km) away, so they hone in with both speed and precision.

In the mid-twentieth century, some of the bald eagles' food sources became toxic. After World War II (1939–1945), materials such as DDT, which had been developed for weapons, were used in pesticides. Farmers in the United States began using increased amounts of these chemicals, and nearby rivers became contaminated with them. Pesticides were also used to control mosquitoes near waterways at this time, which increased contamination. Fish is a staple of bald eagles' diets, and the toxic fish they ate from the contaminated rivers caused their numbers to decline. By 1963, there were only 417 pairs of bald eagles left in the lower 48 United States.[2] Four years later, the government listed bald eagles within that area as endangered. By 1995, the bald eagle's status was lowered to threatened. In 2007, it was estimated that the population in the United States had risen to more than 11,000 pairs, and bald eagles were removed from the threatened list as well.[3]

ANIMALS ON THE PLAINS

Another US animal that neared extinction was the American bison, also commonly called the buffalo. Strong and statuesque, the American bison used to run in herds across the Great Plains in numbers too great to count. It is the largest land animal native to the country, weighing anywhere between 700 and 2,000 pounds (318 and 908 kg).

Commercial hunting of American bison—mostly for its hide—began in the eighteenth century and became prevalent in the nineteenth century, nearly wiping out the entire population of the giant herbivores. By 1885, there were only approximately 500 American bison in the entire nation. But through conservation efforts put in effect since then, these

SPECIES IN DANGER

Awareness of a decline in US animal and plant species populations can be traced to the mid-nineteenth century. In the early twentieth century, conservationists, spurred on by the alarming drop in the population of bison, passenger pigeons, and whooping cranes, pushed the US Congress to take action to save plants and wildlife in danger of extinction. Though some of these conservation efforts started as early as 1905, they did not come to fruition until passage of the Endangered Species Act of 1973. The act prohibited the collecting, capturing, and hunting of species that are protected by the law. This protection has created successful rehabilitation for many species. Several protected species, including the gray wolf, have been removed from the list since the act passed due to dramatic population growth.

animals have made a comeback, with approximately 350,000 in North America.[4]

Bison today are found mostly in publicly protected lands, where the bison are also protected. These lands include Custer State Park in South Dakota, the Henry Mountains in Utah, and Yellowstone National Park. The sight of these giant animals thundering through the plains is an amazing spectacle.

Pronghorns are another animal found in the plains of the West. These quick-footed animals are related to and resemble a goat, and they have large horns. Today, pronghorns can be found in the Great Plains, many western states including Wyoming and Montana, and as far west as parts of California and Oregon. Many other hoofed animals live in the United States, including the white-tailed deer, which can be found throughout the country but mostly live east of the Rocky Mountains, and the black-tailed deer, which are found out West.

The mountain lion, also known as the cougar or puma, also lives out West. However, these animals have been sighted as far east as Missouri and Arkansas. Native to America, cougars can survive in mountainous regions as well as deserts, forests, swamps, and grasslands.

BEARS, MOOSE, AND GATORS

The United States is home to several types of bears. The massive grizzly bear, weighing anywhere from 400 to 800 pounds (182 to 363 kg),

American bison fur is so thick snow sometimes lands on their backs and does not melt.

roams part of the northwestern United States. More commonly seen in the United States is the black bear, which varies in size, with the female weighing between 90 and 370 pounds (41 and 170 kg) and the male weighing between 130 and 550 pounds (59 and 250 kg). As many

A grizzly bear roams the Alaskan wilderness.

as 6,000 polar bears, the largest species of bear in the United States, live in Alaska.[5] Polar bears can grow as large as 1,500 pounds (681 kg) and they have white fur.

Moose are another animal that often live in Alaska, but they have a much larger range than the polar bear. The largest member of the deer family, moose also meander through the upper Rocky Mountains, northeastern Minnesota, the Upper Peninsula of Michigan, northern New England, and even upstate New York.

In addition to the dolphins, manatees, sharks, and fish found in the bordering oceans, the southern coasts host an abundance of animals that are distinct from anywhere else in the nation. Alligators, which are reptiles that can be anywhere from 6 to 14 feet (2 to 4 m) long, are found in the southeastern United States. Many alligators live in Florida, but Louisiana has the largest alligator population in the United States. More than 1 million wild gators live in Louisiana's wetlands.[6]

The United States is host to many other wild animals, including everything from wolves, foxes, beavers, and woodchucks, to snakes, scorpions, seals, and sea turtles. Numerous birds fly the skies as well. In fact, each of the 50 US states has an official state bird.

WOODLANDS AND PLANT LIFE

All 50 US states also have an official state flower. Many of these flowers are native to a particular part of the country. Different native violet species are the state flowers of Wisconsin, Illinois, New Jersey, and Rhode Island. Some state flowers have strong historical associations with their states' history, such as the mayflower in Massachusetts, which was also the name of a ship that transported immigrants and adventurers to that area in the seventeenth century.

Plant life across the nation develops based on climate. Cacti survive and flourish in the hot, arid deserts in the Southwest. Cypress trees have found a home in the South's dampest swamps, and evergreen forests thrive in rain-soaked Oregon and western Washington.

Approximately 33 percent of the land in the United States is forest.[7] These woodlands are home to many trees and plants. Northern forests are dominated by birch, maple, oak, and hickory trees, while pines predominate in the South and ponderosa pines and Douglas firs are prevalent in the West. Twenty percent of forestland is protected by conservation efforts.[8] Cutting down trees for commercial use or to prevent the spread of insects, disease, and invasive weeds can pose threats to natural forest life.

ENVIRONMENTAL THREATS AND PROTECTION

The uncontrolled use of open spaces and wilderness to house an ever-growing human population is a growing environmental concern in the United States. The federal government has been hesitant to regulate how local communities develop land. Loss of open space due to human expansion in the form of commercial and residential building can damage or wipe out plant life, natural springs and streams, and even wildlife living in formerly untouched areas.

A forest of birch and other trees in northern Wisconsin

With human expansion also comes more air and water pollution. The increased use of fossil fuels, such as oil and coal, by people for energy worsens climate change, which threatens sustainability for the nation's plants and animals.

To protect the country's critical habitats and animals that live within them, 58 national parks have been established. Among the most notable are Yellowstone, Grand Canyon, Yosemite, and Olympic National Parks. Located in the rugged plains of Wyoming, Yellowstone was the world's first national park. Sixty-seven species of animals and 1,500 species of native plants live within the park's vast 3,472 square miles (8,992 sq km).[8] Forests of pine trees surround natural spectacles including nearly 300 waterfalls, an active volcano, geysers, and more.

The namesake feature of Grand Canyon National Park in Arizona is a breathtaking gorge one mile (1.6 km) deep formed by the Colorado River. Nearly 5 million visitors trek to this park each year to view the vast beauty of the walls of the canyon,

SEQUOIA TREES

The giant sequoia trees found in California's Sierra Nevada Mountain Range, including Yosemite National Park and Sequoia National Park, are considered a national treasure. The only sequoias left on earth, some of these trees are 3,000 years old. A natural wood preservative in sequoias that is resistant to disease is one of the reasons for the trees' longevity. Sequoia trees can grow to be 300 feet (91 m) tall and 30 feet (9 m) across. It is illegal to cut them down.

tinted in deep ambers, browns, and reds.[9] The giant sequoia trees in California's Yosemite National Park are quite a sight as well. The towering timbers overlook the park from several hundred feet and can live for thousands of years. Among the sequoias here are rivers, granite cliffs, and over 400 species of animals, including two that are thought to only exist within Yosemite National Park.[10]

Olympic National Park in Washington is yet another conserved space that reflects the nation's diversity and beauty. Lush forests, snowcapped mountain peaks, moss-framed

ENDANGERED SPECIES IN THE UNITED STATES

According to the International Union for Conservation of Nature (IUCN), the United States is home to many species that are categorized by the organization as Critically Endangered, Endangered, or Vulnerable:

Mammals	37
Birds	76
Reptiles	36
Amphibians	56
Fishes	183
Mollusks	268
Other Invertebrates	258
Plants	243
Total	1,157[11]

waterfalls, and 3,000 miles (4,800 km) of rivers and streams cut through the park's landscape.

The National Parks Conservation Association works to protect the natural beauty found in all national parks in the United States. It also educates the public and government on park conservation, upholds laws protecting the parks, and generally ensures that these testaments to the nation's history and unique geographic diversity remain intact.

National parks such as Yosemite protect the nation's abundant forests, natural waterways, and diverse species.

CHAPTER 4

HISTORY: PRESERVING FREEDOM

Experts estimate that the first people to inhabit the land that would become the United States crossed a strip of land and ice that linked northeastern Asia with Alaska 20,000 years ago. These early settlers, known as Paleo-Indians, established a society in the New World that was built around farming, hunting, and fishing. These people are the ancestors of Native Americans.

NATIVE AMERICANS

By the mid-fifteenth century, it is estimated that as many as 10 million Native Americans lived north of Mexico in the Americas.[1] They survived off the land as farmers and hunters and made the most

For many centuries, the Native American population grew rapidly.

of their surroundings, developing tools, homes, and clothing from natural materials.

There were distinct tribes, or groups, of Native Americans. They lived in communities with their own languages and leaders and had their own traditions. There were approximately 375 distinct Native American languages.[2] There was a significant amount of trade and migration, but certain Native American tribes put down roots in particular locales. Native Americans believed the land belonged to everyone in the community. No individual owned land.

EARLY COLONIZATION

In 1492, Italian explorer Christopher Columbus came upon the island of Hispaniola in the Caribbean. He was not the first European to reach American shores, but his visit opened the way to a flood of European colonists and explorers. Spaniards built the initial colonies in the New World—first in Saint Augustine in 1565, in what is now Florida, then in approximately 1607 in Santa Fe, on land that became New Mexico. Other explorers came to the New World shortly after Columbus, including explorers from Britain. British colonists began building permanent settlements in the early seventeenth century.

The Spanish had been settling the New World for decades before the British built their first colonies.

Britain put down permanent roots in what came to be known as America in 1607, when 100 people started a British colony in Jamestown on the mid-Atlantic coast. In 1620, a group of Pilgrims, people who went to the New World in search of religious freedom, settled in Plymouth, approximately 500 miles (800 km) north of Jamestown along the Atlantic coast. More European settlers arrived throughout the seventeenth century and eventually set up a string of colonies along the Atlantic coast.

Without regard for the indigenous population, European settlers forced Native Americans off their land. In addition, these settlers unintentionally introduced infectious diseases nonexistent among the Native Americans, and for which they had no immunity. Many Native Americans died as a result, which only further aided the European conquest of the area.

By the 1730s, the British Empire included 13 colonies in America on the East Coast. British colonists started moving westward. They ran into and fought with French trappers, who traded along the Mississippi River, and they also clashed with multiple tribes of Native Americans, who refused to be ousted from their land.

These conflicts led to the French and Indian War in 1754. French soldiers, allied with some Native American tribes and some Spaniards, tried to curb British expansion in the New World. Colonial militia and British soldiers won the French and Indian War in 1763. France lost most

As a colonel, George Washington led soldiers during the French and Indian War.

of its land claims east of the Mississippi River, and the Native Americans living on land formerly governed by France now came under British rule. British leaders were less willing to stop British settlers from taking over Native American lands.

The British Parliament imposed a series of taxes on the colonies to pay for the cost of their defense, which led to widespread protests in America. This eventually led to armed conflict in 1775, which was the start of the American Revolutionary War. The Continental Congress, which consisted of delegates from the colonies, decided to cut ties with Great Britain and issued the Declaration of Independence on July 4, 1776. The American Revolution lasted until 1783, taking a heavy toll on the colonies but establishing a free nation: the United States of America.

Delegates drafted a Constitution on how the new nation was to be governed. A strong central government was proposed in the Constitution, with a separation of powers among branches and between the federal government and the states. The Constitution became the law of the land in 1788. General George Washington was elected president in 1789 and left office in 1797 after two four-year terms. John Adams became the nation's second president.

GOING WEST

In 1803, Thomas Jefferson, who succeeded Adams as president, purchased 828,000 square miles (2,145,000 sq km) of the Louisiana Territory from France. Known as the Louisiana Purchase, the land included part or all of 15 new states, stretching west from the Mississippi River to the Rocky Mountains. The Louisiana Purchase set the stage for the nation to grow all the way to the West Coast. To learn more about the purchased land, Jefferson put together the Corps of Discovery Expedition, led by Meriwether Lewis and William Clark. Accompanied by a 31-member team, including a female Native American scout named Sacagawea, Lewis and Clark's journey took more than two years (1804–1806).

PUSHING WEST

Settling the West led to numerous conflicts with Native Americans who lived on land across the nation's Great Plains and the Southwest for generations. The US Army pushed many Native Americans off their land. Major fighting stopped in 1891, but sporadic armed conflicts with Native Americans lasted until the early 1920s. Many tribes were displaced and relocated to reservations, where they were confined and controlled by the US government. Many reservations remain today, and are run by Native American tribes within the bounds of state and federal law. The relocation and westward takeover of the nation's native people is a controversial topic to many regarding US history.

By 1812, several contributing factors, including trade restrictions imposed by Great Britain against the United States, led to a war. The War of 1812 lasted two and a half years. It came to an end with the signing of the Treaty of Ghent, in which Britain agreed to evacuate US territory, thereby lifting all trading restrictions.

SLAVERY

The first black slaves from Africa were forcibly brought to Jamestown as early as 1619. Many were transported to the New World after that through what was known as the "triangular trade." Ships from England brought goods to the West African Coast, where goods were traded for Africans who had been abducted. The kidnapped Africans were then taken to the Americas, where they were traded for goods and sold into slavery. Ships then returned to England, loaded with goods such as sugar, tobacco, and cotton, completing the triangle of trade.

In 1808, the importation of slaves was banned, but slavery itself was not. The 13 British colonies that became the United States were heavily involved in slave trading—the southern ones much more than those in the North. Much of the South's economy was based on the forced free labor of slaves. The practice was still legal in southern states in the 1850s, but mostly outlawed in northern states. By the 1860s, there were still approximately 4 million slaves in the South.[3]

Politician Abraham Lincoln was against slavery spreading to the new western territories. He opposed the Kansas-Nebraska Act of 1854, which let settlers decide whether slavery should be allowed, rather than having Congress decide. The act led to violence as both pro- and antislavery settlers descended on Kansas and clashed over the issue.

On November 6, 1860, Lincoln won the presidency, and Southern states started leaving the Union before he even took office. Eleven states eventually left the Union and formed the Confederacy: Alabama, Florida,

Georgia, Louisiana, Mississippi, South Carolina, North Carolina, Virginia, Arkansas, Tennessee, and Texas.

The Civil War between the Union and the Confederacy began on April 12, 1861, and an extremely bitter conflict ensued. It is commonly estimated at least 620,000 lives were lost, but some claim the total count may be nearly 100,000 higher.[4] Robert E. Lee, the leader of the Confederate troops, surrendered on April 9, 1865, ending the war. However, Southern sympathizer John Wilkes Booth assassinated President Lincoln on April 14. The Union's victory put an end to the Confederacy and to slavery in the United States.

All the Confederate states were eventually readmitted to the Union, but the South suffered great physical and financial damage as a result of the Civil War. In an effort to rebuild the South and gain equal rights for African Americans, a period of

ABOLISHING SLAVERY

On January 1, 1863, President Lincoln issued the Emancipation Proclamation, freeing all the slaves living in Confederate states. To ensure slavery would never return, he and other Republicans in Congress pushed to abolish it through a constitutional amendment. In December 1865, the Thirteenth Amendment to the Constitution was adopted, eliminating slavery forever. Two companion amendments—the Fourteenth and Fifteenth—extended some additional rights to African Americans. Ending slavery, however, did not give equal rights to African Americans. Equal rights for African Americans were not established for 100 more years, until the civil rights movement of the 1960s.

Reconstruction in the South followed the war from 1865 to 1877. Undermined by political corruption and greed, Reconstruction ultimately failed to bring about lasting reform, especially in equal rights. The result was a segregated South with the white majority passing laws to restrict the rights of freed slaves.

INDUSTRIALIZATION

Before the Civil War, the North was in the midst of the Industrial Revolution. After the war, the entire country converted to an industrial economy, and vast numbers of immigrants, mostly from Europe, made their way to the United States seeking jobs. The nation also needed improved transportation, and that meant expanding railroad systems.

The most ambitious transportation construction project in the country was the first Transcontinental Railroad, built between 1863 and 1869. The railroad linked the East with the West and cut through a great deal of western acreage, spawning new towns in its wake. However, the construction destroyed vast, open plains and displaced Native Americans. It also caused bison populations to dwindle, first being hunted for workers' food, and then when wearing buffalo hide became fashionable.

Starting in the late nineteenth century, the United States sold more of its goods overseas, developing a global economy and becoming a world power. The turn of the twentieth century marked a period of major social and political reform in the United States, known as the Progressive

Era. Activists worked to rid government of the public corruption that had become entrenched during the late nineteenth century.

Progressives sought change in public education, health care, insurance, poverty, child labor, industry, food standards, and women's suffrage. They battled alcohol abuse and succeeded in banning alcohol through the Eighteenth Amendment in 1919, which ushered in the controversial period known as Prohibition.

When World War I (1914–1918) broke out in Europe in 1914, many Americans wanted to stay out of the conflict. Germany tested the United States' resolve of nonintervention by sending submarines to attack and sink US merchant ships. The United States finally entered the war on April 6, 1917, and sent 2 million troops to Europe to bolster the Allied war effort. The war ended on November 11, 1918, with a victory for the United States and its allies.

WOMEN'S RIGHTS

On July 19, 1848, in a hot, stuffy church in Seneca Falls, New York, 240 people, including 40 men, met to discuss a series of resolutions calling for equal rights for women. The event became known as the Seneca Falls Convention. Each of the resolutions was debated, including a woman's right to vote. Many at the convention thought the proposal was simply too radical for the time. But Elizabeth Cady Stanton, who proposed the resolution, stood her ground. It was passed by the convention. In the years following the convention, women ran a tireless campaign for equal rights. Women did not gain the right to vote in all elections for another 72 years, until the Nineteenth Amendment to the US Constitution was ratified in 1920.

The decade following, 1920 to 1929, became known as the Roaring Twenties. It was a period of economic prosperity and cultural renaissance in the United States, especially concerning music and dance.

THE GREAT DEPRESSION

In the 1920s, more goods were manufactured than the consumer market could absorb, and people spent money frivolously. The economic bubble burst with the stock market crash in October 1929, signaling the start of the Great Depression in the United States. Financial woes led to the worst unemployment in the nation's history. The Great Depression coincided with the Dust Bowl in the southern plains, a seven-year period of below-normal rainfall on the heels of aggressive agricultural practices, which led to famine. This downturn led to a worldwide slump, as many other nations had developed economic ties with the United States.

Those who sold alcohol were among the few who did not suffer financial setbacks during the Depression. Alcohol sales and consumption were banned under Prohibition until 1933, but consumers were willing to buy alcohol illegally. By the late 1920s, diminishing support for Prohibition led to its repeal through the Twenty-first Amendment, ratified in 1933. Also that year, Franklin D. Roosevelt became president and made meaningful steps through a program called the New Deal to offer economic relief from the Great Depression.

Homeless or unemployed people line up to receive free bread in New York City during the Great Depression.

US MILITARY CASUALTIES OF WAR

American Revolution	4,435
War of 1812	2,260
Civil War	364,511
World War I	116,516
World War II	405,399
Korean War	36,574
Vietnam War	58,209
Persian Gulf War	382[6]
Iraq War	4,477 (as of February 2012)[7]
War in Afghanistan	1,888 (as of February 2012)[8]

World War II began in 1939, but the United States did not get involved until 1941. On December 7 of that year, Japan launched a surprise attack on a US naval base in Pearl Harbor, Hawaii. It is approximated more than 2,400 people were killed.[5] The United States declared war on Japan and Japan's ally, Germany.

Germany surrendered on April 29, 1945. But war with Japan continued for a few more months. The United States dropped two atomic bombs—one on the Japanese city of Hiroshima on August 6, and the other on Nagasaki on August 9. It is estimated those two atomic bombs—the only use of nuclear weapons in war to date—killed more than 200,000 people and inflicted countless injuries.[9] Japan surrendered on August 15. The war ended in a victory for the United States and its allies.

BOOM TIMES

World War II put an end to the Great Depression in the United States. Many returning soldiers settled down in the suburbs of major cities, and the housing market boomed. Many who served in the armed forces decided to take advantage of a government program that gave them the opportunity to go to college.

Although the economy was rehabilitated, threats to world peace were not over. The United States entered the Cold War era, a time of military and political tension between the United States and the Soviet Union. The conflicting ideologies between the two countries never led to them fighting each other directly, but each took opposing sides in military conflicts around the world, supplying troops and weapons to the side it favored. These included the Korean and Vietnam Wars.

The Vietnam War was in its early stages in 1960 when John F. Kennedy took office as president. Kennedy visualized many goals for the nation but was assassinated on November 22, 1963. The nation fulfilled one of Kennedy's ambitious goals, for space exploration, on July 20, 1969, when the United States landed a man on the moon.

Martin Luther King Jr. gave his famed "I Have a Dream" speech on racial equality on August 28, 1963.

CIVIL RIGHTS

African Americans began battling segregation long before the 1950s, but it was in this decade that activists amplified the legal challenges to segregation. Known as the civil rights movement, the fight for equal rights for African Americans was spearheaded by Martin Luther King Jr. One milestone of the movement was the passage of the Civil Rights Act of 1964. The act banned discrimination based on race, religion, or national origin.

At the same time, Native Americans began pressing for recognition of their rights through the American Indian Movement. Its goal was to get the US government to rectify past injustices inflicted against Native Americans.

THE END OF THE CENTURY

The nation was divided over the unpopular involvement in the war in Vietnam when Richard Nixon was elected president in 1968. President Nixon said he had a plan to end the war, but his efforts to do so were overshadowed by a political cover-up scandal in the White House called Watergate.

Through the 1980s and 1990s, the United States maintained its prowess as the world's financial and military superpower. The nation was involved in the brief Persian Gulf War (1990–1991) that was started by Iraq's invasion of Kuwait on August 2, 1990. A US-led coalition launched an attack on Iraq on January 17, 1991 and, with superior US military technology, Kuwait was liberated some six weeks later.

TERRORISM

Nearing the dawn of the twenty-first century, the nation experienced domestic and international terrorism. A shocking 1995 bombing of the federal building in Oklahoma City, Oklahoma, killed 168 innocent people. More shocking was the discovery that it was an act of domestic terrorism: the bomber was a US citizen.

Then on September 11, 2001, international terrorists hijacked four jetliners with passengers onboard. They flew two of the planes into the World Trade Center towers in New York City. Another plane was flown into the Pentagon building in Washington DC, and onboard struggles between terrorists and passengers led the fourth to crash into a field in Shanksville, Pennsylvania. Nearly 3,000 people in total were killed in the attacks, which came to be known as 9/11.[10] In response, the United States sent troops into Afghanistan, a nation known to harbor al-Qaeda, the terrorist group responsible for the attacks. The Afghanistan War ensued and continued as of 2012. The United States became involved in another war, the Iraq War, during this time as well, which continued until 2011. Both wars became highly controversial with the US media and citizens.

Despite the conflicts and controversy throughout the nation's history, the American dream has continued to survive. The United States remains the land of opportunity, where, with hard work and determination, anything is possible.

A second terrorist-controlled plane approached the smoking World Trade Center on September 11, 2001, which was hit moments before by a first plane.

CHAPTER 5

PEOPLE:
A COMMON BOND

As a whole, the collective spirit of the people of the United States has helped make the country a leader in science, technology, medicine, business, entertainment, education, social awareness, and humanitarian efforts. A compassionate nature and abundance of opportunity defines and creates a common bond between the many people that make up the nation's unique population.

The majority of the US population are urban dwellers. Some 250 million people reside in or very near cities in the United States.[1] That means approximately three-quarters of the US population live on 3 percent of its land.[2] People make their homes close to cities because most urban areas offer jobs, mass transportation, cultural and sporting events, and a wide selection of fine dining and entertainment. With an estimated population of more than 19.3 million as of July 2009,

The American people are diverse but often come together in times of crisis and need to help one another.

OWNING A HOME

Many US citizens still have the American dream of owning their own homes, but fewer can do it today. Only 62 percent of the population owns their own homes now, a drop from 73 percent just five years ago. These numbers are further broken down by ethnicity. Close to 75 percent of Caucasians and 59 percent of Asian Americans had their own homes according to 2010 data.[12] Those who identified themselves as Hispanic had a home ownership rate of approximately 48 percent, while a little more than 45 percent of African Americans had a deed to their residence.[13]

the New York City area has more residents than any other metropolis in the country.[3] The large states of California and Texas are the most populous. California's population is more than 37 million.[4] Texas has approximately 25 million people.[5]

The nation has the third-largest population in the world with more than 313 million people.[6] Of the overall US population, more than one-quarter of all the people in the country are under 20 years old.[7] The average age is 36.9 years old.[8] Thirteen percent of the population is over 65.[9] Life expectancy is currently at 78 years, an all-time high for the nation. Women typically outlive men by approximately five years.[10] In the overall population of the United States, women outnumber men by more than 5 million.[11]

Most people living in the United States are Caucasian—close to 80 percent. African Americans make up 12.85 percent of all inhabitants. Asians comprise another 4.43 percent. Amerindian and Alaska Natives

Population Density of the United States

comprise close to 1 percent, and native Hawaiian and Pacific Islanders 0.18 percent. People that are two or more races make up 1.61 percent. The Hispanic community can include people from Mexico, Cuba, Puerto Rico, the Dominican Republic, Spain, Central America, and South America that are any race. These people account for 15.1 percent of the populace and are the fastest-growing segment of the population.[14]

A NATION OF IMMIGRANTS

Immigrants are a part of American history. After the Native Americans, early settlers to North America came from England, Spain, Germany, and the Netherlands. French, Irish, and Scandinavians followed soon afterward. The United States became a melting pot of ethnicity, a term often used to describe the culture even today.

In the early eighteenth century, inhabitants hailed from many countries and spoke many languages other than English. From then on, the country developed to include a wide-ranging mix of people with diverse backgrounds. The cultures of these settlers were incorporated into the nation, along with the Native American cultures that had been established thousands of years before European colonization started. Native Americans still live all over the country, including in Alaska and Hawaii. One-third of the 2.8 million Native Americans in the United States today live in California, Oklahoma, and Arizona.[15]

The US population is comprised of many different races and ethnicities.

YOU SAY IT!

English	Spanish	Hawaiian
Hello	Hola (OH-la)	Aloha (AH-loh-ha)
Good-bye	Adiós (ah-dee-OHS)	Aloha (AH-loh-ha)
Good Morning	Buenos Días (booEHN-os DEE-as)	Aloha Kakahiaka (AH-loh-ha kah-kah-HEE-ah-kah)
Name	Nombre (NOHM-breh)	Inoa (ee-NOH-ah)
Friend	Amigo (ah-MEE-go)	Hoaaloha (hoh-AH-loh-ha)
Today	Hoy (OY)	Keia La (KAY-ee-ah LAH)
Thank You	Gracias (grah-SEE-us)	Mahalo (mah-HAH-loh)
Yes	Sí (SEE)	Ae (EYE)
No	No (NO)	A'ole (AH-oh-lay)

Of the many cultural groups represented in the United States, English is the native language of more than 82 percent of the people.[16] However, although 28 states have passed legislation giving English "official language" status, the country has no official language.[17] Many other languages are spoken in the United States and used in official documents.

For example, Spanish is spoken by 10 percent of the population.[18] In areas where Spanish is prevalent, including parts of the West, Southwest, Florida, and urban areas in the Northeast, many documents, including voting ballots, government forms, ordinances, and emergency safety instructions, are provided in Spanish as well as English. A similar approach is taken where there are large populations of other non-English speakers, such as Koreans, Vietnamese, and Thais in parts of California, and Chinese in King County in the state of Washington, among others. Forty-four states offer written driver's license exams in languages other than English. Massachusetts offers the exam in 25 languages, New York in 22, and California in 21.[19]

Approximately 20 percent of the US population is bilingual.

It is estimated that more than 350 languages are spoken in the United States.[20] In addition to legal documents, some businesses and professional services, such as doctors, lawyers, and accountants, try to make bilingual staff available for consumers. The additional costs associated with multilingualism, such as staffing and printing, however, are a growing issue. Multilingualism also puts financial pressure on the public

POLLING PLACE
VOTE HERE
VOTE AQUI
LUGAR PARA
VOTAR
在此投票
投票站
BỎ PHIẾU TẠI ĐÂY
PHÒNG PHIẾU

education system. Those without a solid grasp of the English language have a harder time succeeding in the United States. They find it especially difficult to get good-paying jobs.

The United States has not always welcomed people from foreign lands with open arms. The Chinese came to the US West Coast—primarily California—during the gold rush in 1849, and an anti-Chinese sentiment developed in the United States. By 1882, Congress passed the Chinese Exclusion Act, banning

IMMIGRATION BY REGION[21]

Approximately 40 million US residents were born in a foreign country as of 2010. Most came from Latin America. Here is the breakdown:

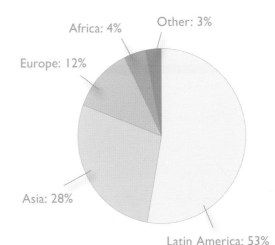

Other: 3%
Africa: 4%
Europe: 12%
Asia: 28%
Latin America: 53%

A multilingual sign at the Santa Clara County Office of the Registrar of Voters lists information in English, Spanish, Vietnamese, and Chinese.

Chinese immigration for ten years. The ban was eventually extended and was not lifted until 1943.

In the early 1900s, nativism was spreading rapidly throughout the country. When 805,000 immigrants made their way to the United States from other parts of the world in 1921, the issue boiled over. A quota system was set up in 1921, limiting the number of immigrants who could enter the country legally. It was aimed at curbing European immigration, but there was a ban on Japanese immigration, causing tension between the two nations. The quotas did not apply to immigrants from countries in the Western Hemisphere, such as Canada and Mexico.

The US Census Bureau predicted in 2000 that the nation's population would double in 100 years.

The United States enforced the quota system until 1965. US immigration laws have been revised many times in recent decades. But these efforts have failed to resolve the issue, and the nation continues to grapple with illegal immigration.

More illegal immigrants now enter the United States than those who follow the formal legal process to enter the country. It is estimated that 11 million illegal aliens live in the United States. Sixty percent of those entering the United States illegally come from Mexico, 20 percent from Latin America, and 11 percent from Asia.[22] Elected officials in the United States fiercely debate the impact of illegal immigration. There are several arguing points, but the debate centers around illegal aliens often being willing to work for lower wages and therefore being hired for jobs instead of US citizens, who desire higher pay. The cost to government for providing social services and health care when required to these individuals is another controversial issue.

A MECCA FOR RELIGIOUS FREEDOM

Religious freedom was a founding principle of the United States and one reason many settlers first came to the New World. Today, people of all religions coexist in the United States, and, in general, respect each others' religious beliefs and right to worship as they please or not worship at all.

Much of the predicted US population growth is expected to come from future immigration.

Religion is an important part of many people's lives in the United States. Religious leaders often play important roles in their communities. Houses of worship often serve as recreation, learning, and community centers. Many religious organizations assist the sick and less fortunate and fill community needs by running soup kitchens and food pantries, for example.

Some people are so fascinated by religion they not only practice their own religion but they learn about the teachings of other faiths. Interfaith gatherings and fellowship are sometimes encouraged by certain religions. Some of the biggest religious groups are Protestant (51.3 percent), Roman Catholic (23.9 percent), other Christian (1.6 percent), Jewish (1.7 percent), Mormon (1.7 percent), Buddhist (0.7 percent), and Muslim (0.6 percent). All others (18.6 percent) are

recognized as other, unspecified, or unaffiliated.[23] Although there are many faiths practiced in the United States, the nation does not have an official religion.

An imam (Islamic leader), *left*, and rabbi (Jewish leader), *right*, shake hands during a religious tolerance event in Philadelphia, Pennsylvania.

CHAPTER 6

CULTURE: REFLECTIONS OF A NATION

A reflection of the nation where it was invented, baseball has a fan base with people of every race, religion, and background. Reports of baseball being played reach as far back as the 1830s. The sport has provided Americans recreation and joy, but it also served as the moral conscience of the nation when it challenged racial segregation in the mid-1940s. The first African American accepted in the modern major leagues was Jackie Robinson, who made outstanding plays and was accepted by his teammates. His admittance in 1947 contributed significantly to the civil rights movement.

In addition to baseball, many other sports dominate US culture. Professional, college, and high school football engages many communities

American culture celebrates baseball as a career, pastime, and passion.

around the nation. Basketball was invented in Springfield, Massachusetts, with a soccer ball and two peach baskets. Golf, auto racing, tennis, hockey, boxing, and horse racing are also embraced by fans and athletes in the United States. Sports professionals in the United States earn the highest salaries of any athletes in the world.[1] Many are held in high esteem and reach celebrity status, which often remains even after they retire.

The United States has sent competitive athletes to the modern Olympic Games every year since 1896, with the exception of 1980, when the country boycotted the Summer Games in Moscow, Russia, for political reasons. Recently, approximately 600 competitors represented the nation at the 2012 Summer Games in London, England, in 31 different sports including archery, basketball, diving, fencing, judo, swimming, tennis, and wrestling.

COMMERCIAL RADIO

Long before television, people across the United States were entertained by radio. The first commercial radio broadcasts aired in 1920. Putting a broadcast on the air could be costly. So in 1922, radio station WEAF in New York City decided to get businesses involved to lower the cost of putting a show on the radio. In exchange for funding, a WEAF announcer would mention the name of the business during the show. This was how the concept of the commercial was born.

MUSIC AND THEATER

The United States has produced legendary rock and roll, jazz, country western, and hip-hop music through the years. Iconic US singers include

Frank Sinatra, Tony Bennett, Elvis Presley, Barbra Streisand, Michael Jackson, Bruce Springsteen, Whitney Houston, and Aretha Franklin.

The songs of many US composers, which include those by Irving Berlin and George Gershwin from the 1920s and 1930s, are still played today. Many composers in the United States wrote songs for the musical stage. But American theater has put out many memorable tunes as well. In addition to musicals, dramatic plays have long been a mainstay of Broadway, the famous theater district of New York. Many popular plays and musicals have been staged in major cities as well as local community theaters throughout the country.

JAZZ MUSIC

Jazz is a unique American sound born at the turn of the twentieth century. The roots of jazz are found in both European and African music. African-American US musicians first introduced the world to jazz. Many of them were self-taught instrumentalists. Their rhythmic sound was first played in African-American communities throughout the southern United States. Clubs throughout New Orleans, Louisiana, became home to this swinging musical entertainment played by both large dance bands and small ensembles. The city remains an important locale for jazz musicians and fans today.

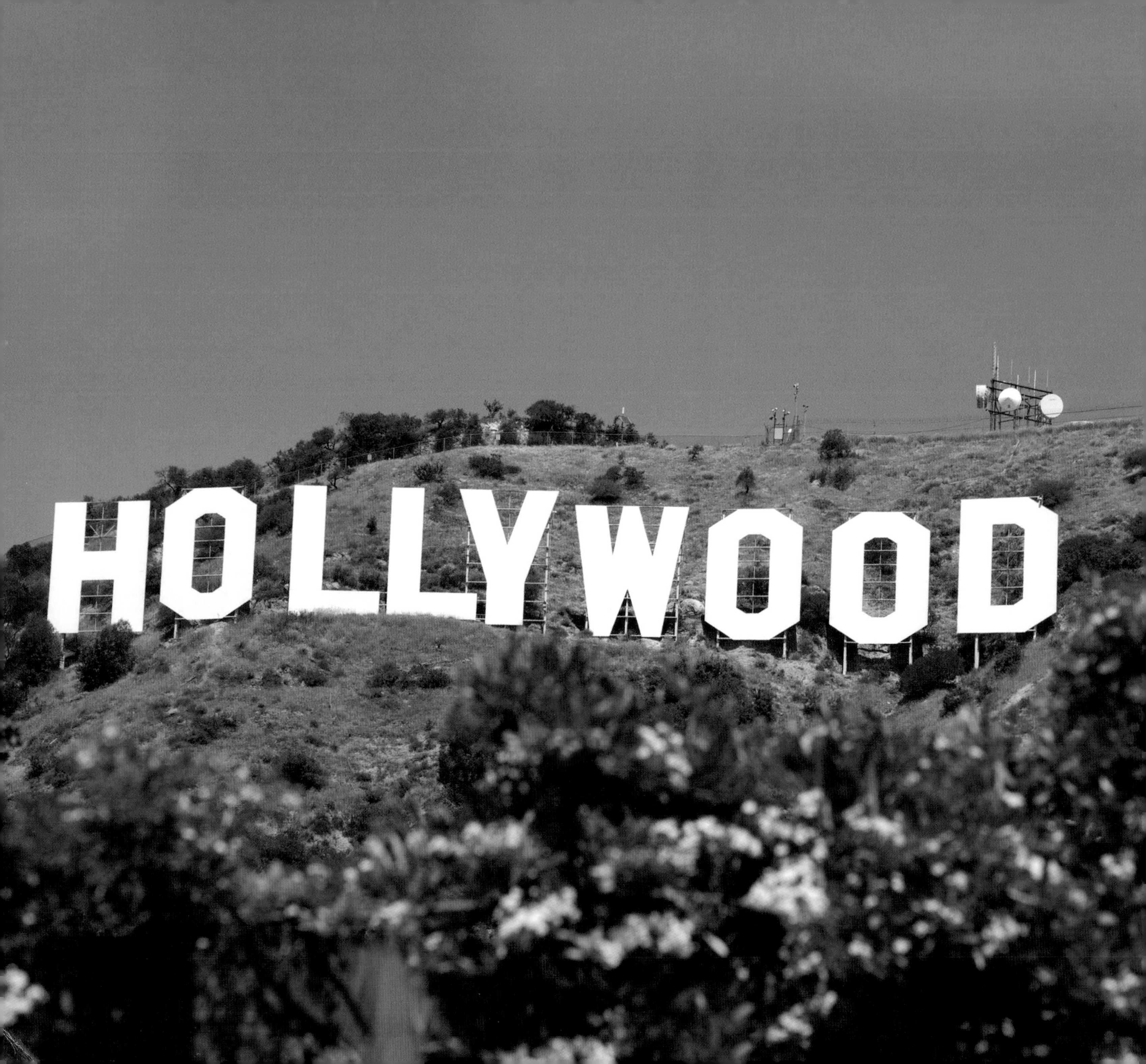
HOLLYWOOD

MOVIES AND TELEVISION

The American public has long flocked to movie theaters, first to view silent films from 1895 to 1929, and then to films with spoken dialogue. Filmmaking put Hollywood, California, on the map. It became the center of the US film industry in the 1930s. Comedies, dramas, musicals, and mysteries all filled the big screen. Many movies have been credited with introducing or encouraging fads in all aspects of American culture, including behavior, slang, dance, cars, hairstyles, and fashion.

Television, known as the small screen, has had just as much influence on American life and attitudes as movies. Coming into its own in the 1950s, television often centered on people's lives, and viewers, in turn, mimicked what they saw on television. Both film and television made stars out of many performers and still do today.

FASCINATION WITH FAME

Fame fascinates the American public. In 1968, American pop artist Andy Warhol said, "In the future, everyone will be world-famous for fifteen minutes."[2] Reality television and the Internet are starting to make Warhol's comment partially come true. With the ability to put just about anything they want on the Internet, people from all walks of life are trying to claim their 15 minutes of fame and turn it into a ticket to success. In the long run, staying power over decades—not minutes—ensures a person's place in American culture.

The Hollywood Sign overlooks the southern California town that grew to be a world-famous film and television hub.

LITERATURE

Classics of American literature span a wide range of genres. US author Mark Twain explored nineteenth-century life along the Mississippi and offered social commentary in *The Adventures of Huckleberry Finn* (1885). A Western theme characterizes the work of many US authors, including Zane Grey, who wrote the best-selling *Riders of the Purple Sage* (1912). John Steinbeck spotlighted the desperate circumstances of families during the Great Depression in *The Grapes of Wrath* (1939). Harper Lee's *To Kill a Mockingbird* (1960) focuses on racial prejudice. Other genres include short stories by F. Scott Fitzgerald, gothic novels such as Stephenie Meyer's *Twilight* series, Stephen King's many horror fiction books, and thrillers such as John Grisham's gripping suspense and crime novels.

SUPERHEROES AND COMIC BOOKS

American writers have created many memorable characters, including incredible superheroes found in the nation's comic books. Comic books first appeared in the United States in 1933. Superman, who debuted in Action Comics in 1938, gave the comic book industry a jolt and launched the nation's admiration and affection for superhero characters. Today, superheroes appear not only in comic books but also on television, in movies and computer games, and as all kinds of marketable products, including plastic action figures.

CARS AND FAST FOOD

Fast, flashy cars have long been part of American culture. Burning up US
roads today are many homegrown sports cars. The Chevrolet Corvette
is perhaps the best-known sports car in the United States. This may be

due in part to one of the most famous advertising taglines in US history, which aimed to sum up American culture in a few words: "Baseball, hot dogs, apple pie, and Chevrolet."[3]

Hot dogs were one of the first fast foods in the nation. German immigrant Charles Feltman sold sausages on rolls in Coney Island, New York, as far back as the 1860s. But hot dogs were being sold in other parts of the country as well, especially at fairs and amusement parks. Quickly made and sold in quick transactions, these hot dogs paved the way for the country to become a fast-food nation.

The first hamburger chain to open in the United States was White Castle in 1921.

The incorporation of fast-food franchises in the United States began in the early 1900s. Many were based on an American favorite, meat and potatoes, served in the form of hamburgers and French fries. More varied menus, featuring ethnic foods representing the diverse population of the United States, are in abundance throughout the country today, especially in major cities.

HOLIDAYS

One of the nation's major holidays is Independence Day, or the Fourth of July, which celebrates the nation's inception during the signing

A sea of people in Seattle, Washington, watch fireworks to celebrate the Fourth of July.

REASON TO CELEBRATE

In addition to federal holidays and ethnic and cultural holidays, the United States has a number of other observances held on special days.

Observance	Purpose	Month
Groundhog Day	predict the weather for the following six weeks	February
Valentine's Day	celebrate love	February
Earth Day	promote ecology	April
National Arbor Day	plant trees	April
Mother's Day	honor and appreciate mothers	May
Father's Day	honor and appreciate fathers	June
Flag Day	salute the flag	June
Halloween	dress in costume, celebrate fright	October

of the Declaration of Independence on July 4, 1776. The Fourth of July is one of ten annual federal holidays. A federal holiday means government offices and many other businesses are closed for the day. Retail stores, however, are open on most federal holidays and do brisk business.

The United States has holidays to honor the military, including Memorial Day in May and Veterans Day in November, and also salutes the nation's leaders on Presidents' Day in February. The efforts of assassinated civil rights leader Martin Luther King Jr. are remembered on his birthday in January every year. Other federal holidays include Labor Day, Columbus Day, Thanksgiving, Christmas, and New Year's Day.

Many immigrants continue to practice cultural traditions from their home countries, including the celebration of holidays. These are not federal holidays, but many festive traditions are observed across the nation to celebrate them. These holidays include the Irish holiday St. Patrick's Day, the Christian holiday of Easter, the Jewish holidays Rosh Hashanah and Yom Kippur, the African-American holiday Kwanzaa, and the Chinese New Year.

Presidents' Day started as an observance of George Washington's birthday.

CHAPTER 7

POLITICS: EVERYONE HAS A VOICE

In simple terms, the United States has a "government of the people, by the people, and for the people."[1] That is how President Lincoln described it during his famous Gettysburg Address in 1863. His words still ring true today.

The United States is still governed by the same Constitution that went into effect shortly after the

OLD GLORY

For many US citizens, the national flag is a source of great pride. The flag flies over all government buildings and often businesses and homes as well. Thirteen alternating red and white horizontal stripes on the flag symbolize the original 13 colonies. A red stripe is always on the top and bottom of the flag. Fifty white, five-pointed stars, representing each of the 50 states, grace a blue rectangle at the upper left corner of the flag. A special day honors the flag every year: Flag Day, which is on June 14.

The US flag has not changed since 1960, when the fiftieth star was added for the state of Hawaii.

nation was founded. The document was originally made up of a preamble and seven articles. It has been amended 27 times in nearly 150 years.

THREE BRANCHES OF GOVERNMENT

The Constitution established a system of checks and balances by creating three individual branches of government. These checks and balances were designed so that no one branch of the government could ever reign supreme. The executive, legislative, and judicial branches each have their own authority, influence, and impact.

The president, who is elected, has the ultimate power in the executive branch of the government. As the nation's chief executive, the president administers, executes, and enforces laws and policy. He is joined in these tasks by the vice president. The president and vice president are members of the same political party, run for office together, and are voted in as a team.

As laid out by the Constitution, the legislative branch is made up of people elected to the House of Representatives and the Senate. The representatives in this branch of the government are collectively called Congress, and they write and pass national laws.

As the government framework was built through developing the Constitution, getting representatives to the Constitutional Convention

Congress meets in the US Capitol Building in Washington DC.

to agree on the legislative structure of the government was a difficult issue. Leaders from states with smaller populations were afraid their states would not be fairly represented. This issue was resolved by the Great Compromise of 1787. Under the agreement, there would be two legislative bodies. The House would have proportional representation—that is, the number of representatives would be based on a state's population. The Senate would have two representatives from each state, no matter how large or small the state was. Today, there are 435 elected members of the House of Representatives and 100 members of the US Senate.

The judicial branch includes the US Supreme Court and the federal court system, which are charged with the responsibility of interpreting the law and

FOUNDING PRINCIPLES

There are several terms used to describe the US government's different systems and processes. *Popular sovereignty* is the belief that the power of the government lies with the people. This power is divided into branches by a separation of powers, which establishes one branch to write the laws (legislative), one branch to implement the laws (executive), and one branch to interpret the laws (judicial). *Judicial review* gives the Supreme Court the power to decide the constitutionality of laws, and *checks and balances* ensure that no one branch of the government becomes too powerful. There is limited government, which means government cannot exceed its authority. The concept that the central government does not have all the power in the nation but that states and municipalities have power as well is known as *federalism*.

making sure it is applied fairly. The federal courts comprise a three-tiered system. A case is first heard by the federal district court. That court's decision can be challenged in federal appeals court and then the US Supreme Court. The US Supreme Court can decide not to hear a case and let the lower court's ruling stand. The federal courts address cases involving the US government, the US Constitution, federal laws, and disputes between the states. They have the right to rule that a law is unconstitutional.

Unlike the president and members of Congress, federal judges are not elected by the people. Instead, they are appointed by the president of the United States and approved by the US Senate. The US Supreme Court has nine justices and is the highest court in the land. Cases that do not involve federal matters are heard in a separate system of municipal and state courts.

THE BILL OF RIGHTS

One of the most important elements of

US SUPREME COURT

When the president of the United States selects someone to serve on the US Supreme Court, it is considered a critical appointment because that person can remain on the court for life. The president can nominate a person for the Supreme Court only when another justice dies, is impeached, resigns, or retires. The president cannot unseat a sitting judge in order to appoint a different judge. Of the nine justices, one is the chief justice; the eight others are associate justices. Each judge votes on the outcome of a case. There are an odd number of judges so rulings do not end in a tie.

STRUCTURE OF THE GOVERNMENT OF THE UNITED STATES

Executive Branch	Legislative Branch	Judicial Branch
President Vice President	House of Representatives Senate	Supreme Court

the US Constitution is the Bill of Rights. However, it was not included when the US Constitution was created. The 55 men who wrote the US Constitution were aware that many state constitutions at the time already had bills of rights, and they did not feel the need to repeat one in the federal document. But its omission was a serious point of dispute.

Many of the framers worried that without a written bill of rights, the national government might abuse its new power and try to erode the very liberties for which the new nation had fought the American Revolution. Those rights included freedom of speech, religion, assembly, press, and the ability to petition the government to right wrongs. The Bill of Rights was adopted in 1791 and comprises the first ten amendments to the Constitution. The bill guarantees citizens personal liberties, which are freedoms the government could never take away. The US

Citizens practice free speech by protesting in front of the White House, which is the president's home and office in Washington DC.

Constitution would probably not have been ratified by the states if the framers had not agreed to add the Bill of Rights.

A TWO-PARTY SYSTEM

While the structure of the US government is established by the Constitution, the political system is not. The United States has a two-party system. The two parties—the Democrats and the Republicans—nominate candidates for political offices on the national, state, and local levels. Those candidates then run for election. In general, the Democratic Party believes government should play a role in alleviating poverty, inequality, and social injustice. The Republican Party favors less government involvement in people's lives, less government spending, and greater individual self-reliance. However, although a two-party system is intact, there is no law limiting the number of political parties in the United States. Smaller parties, often referred to as third parties, sometimes put up candidates to run for public office. Third parties often have a lesser chance of winning an election because they do not have a large following, and the majority of voters support candidates from one of the two major parties. But that is not always the case. One example was in 1998, when Jesse Ventura, a popular retired professional wrestler, ran as a third-party candidate for governor of the state of Minnesota and won.

In a general election, all voters in the United States are free to vote for candidates of any party. US citizens are required to register if they want to vote in elections. Voting is considered a privilege and is not mandatory. No one in the United States is legally required to be a member of a political party. But many people choose to join a political party and get involved in the political process, either running for office or helping campaign for someone who is running for office.

Each of the major political parties includes people with differing views. Both the Democratic and Republican parties are made up of factions, or people with different ideologies. There are times when one faction of the party is in the majority and can set the agenda for that political organization for years to come. It is not unusual for the president of the United States to be from one party while the majority of the Senate and/or House of Representatives are members of the opposition party. This has happened quite a few times in recent years.

GRASSROOTS

Free speech and activism, both safeguarded by the US Constitution, have allowed the United States to make great social advances. Many of these advances were accomplished by citizens who did not hold elective office. Women finally got the right to vote with the passage of the Nineteenth Amendment to the US Constitution in 1920. That was the result of the tireless efforts of Susan B. Anthony and Elizabeth Cady Stanton, who helped lead the charge. The civil rights movement of the mid-twentieth century, led by crusaders such as Dr. Martin Luther King Jr., banned racial discrimination and restored voting rights for African Americans.

President Barack Obama, a Democrat, was elected in 2008. He was reelected in 2012. After that election, the Senate was controlled by Democrats and led by Democratic Senator Harry Reid. The House of Representatives was controlled by the Republicans and led by the House Speaker, Republican John Boehner. When a situation like this occurs, it is called divided government. Elections every two years can change the makeup of Congress, giving the other party power instead.

As of 2011, there were 42 million registered Democrats and 30 million registered Republican voters.

In the past, the art of compromise was the key to getting things accomplished. But the current trend in US politics is gridlock. That means politicians in both parties refuse to work with each other and stall government. Gridlock brings the business of government, such as passing a budget, to a standstill. It has dire consequences, such as shutting down the government, which is a reality in a political world without compromise, and can affect other systems, including the economy.

Barack Obama, the forty-fourth US president

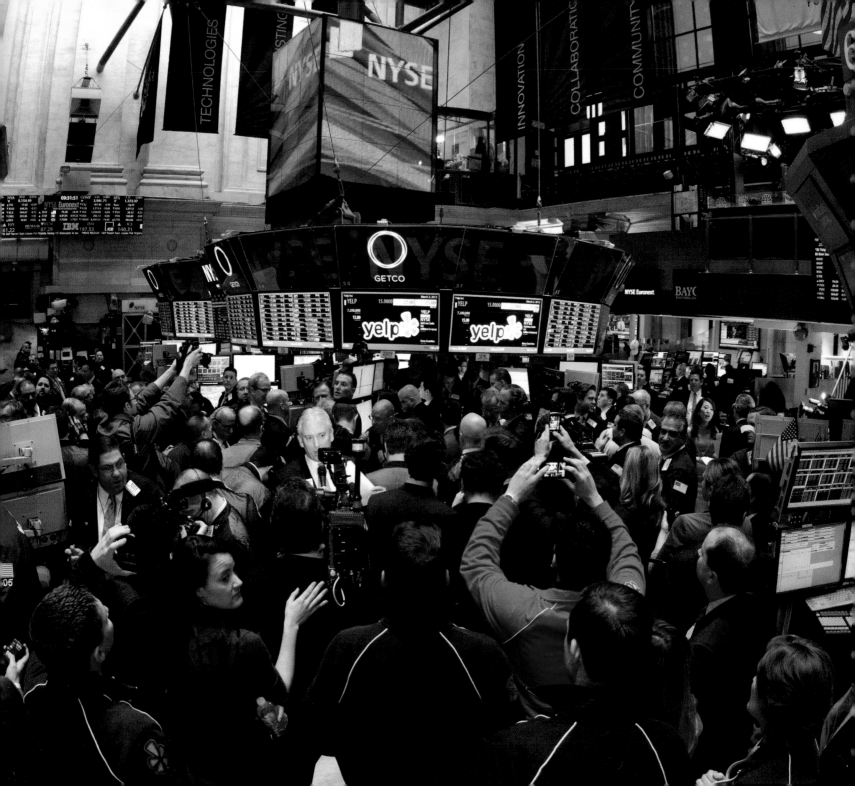

CHAPTER 8

ECONOMICS: HOW THE UNITED STATES WORKS

Every weekday morning at 9:30 a.m., on the floor of the New York Stock Exchange, a bell rings and the United States opens for business. People invest money in various corporations and have a chance to earn a profit at the New York Stock Exchange. It is one of the mainstays of the US economy.

Today, the United States has the largest national economy in the world. Financial institutions such as the New York Stock Exchange are just one aspect of the economy. There are many others, including industry, agriculture, manufacturing, small businesses, professional services, and countless others.

Stock traders working on the floor of the New York Stock Exchange in 2012

Agriculture powered the economy in colonial days and for decades after the United States won independence from Britain. During that time, people grew or made everything they needed. The Industrial Revolution in the nineteenth century propelled the United States toward becoming an economic superpower. Along the way, the economy had its up and downs. The US economic system has gone through recessions, as well as severe depressions. There have also been boom times with quick financial growth, new business start-ups, and robust employment.

Farming still has a role in the US economy today. The nation leads the world in agricultural output. There are 2.2 million farms across the United States.[1] The nation's top agricultural product is corn, and much of the world gets its corn from US farms.[2] Other major farm products include wheat, cow's milk, soybeans, eggs, cotton, and fruits and vegetables.

A SERVICE-ORIENTED ECONOMY

The service industry is one of the nation's top-growing sectors, providing services such as insurance, health care, banking, repairs, cleaning, deliveries, and technology. More than 75 percent of the workforce is employed in the service industry.[3] The service industry developed in the second half of the twentieth century. As wealth increased following the end of World War II in 1945, people could afford to pay for services, especially ones that could make life easier and more convenient, such as telecommunications and lawn care.

Grain crops are a critical US export.

Research and development into new technology and products is another major force in today's economy, but it is not a new concept in the United States. From Alexander Graham Bell's telephone to Thomas Edison's movie camera, called a Kinetograph, Americans have historically sought to create and market clever new products. Research and development today includes scientific discoveries, new products, and pioneering technology.

ENTREPRENEURSHIP

Research and development breakthroughs often lead to entrepreneurship as innovators start new businesses to market their products and ideas. Small businesses employ the largest number of US workers: approximately 53 percent of all jobs.[4] Small companies can often grow into large companies, which are staffed by 38 percent of the workforce.[5] Therefore, creating jobs for small businesses is a driving force in the US economy.

GOVERNMENT PAYROLL

The biggest employer in the nation is the nation itself. With 2.2 million civilian employees, excluding postal workers, the federal government is the country's largest employer. One out of every 66 people works for the federal government. When government workers on all levels—federal, state, and local—are added up, they total 21 million workers.[6]

The transportation industry keeps the United States on the move. In the nation's biggest metropolitan areas, commuter trains, subways, and buses help people reach their destinations. These transportation systems create many jobs, as they require conductors and drivers, as well as people to manage the lines, sell tickets, and perform maintenance and other tasks.

US roads are filled with 250 million motor vehicles.[7] Those cars stimulate economic growth from car manufacturing to car repair and sales. Transportation goods, such as cars and trucks, are leading manufacturing moneymakers today in the United States. There are also workers who maintain the infrastructure around the country so drivers can navigate the roads safely and easily for work and leisure.

Busy airports throughout the United States take people from one part of the country to another and all around the world. Flights can also carry small packages throughout the country and overseas. The overnight package delivery business enables US companies to ship products to customers faster than ever before. Heavy freight is shipped by land, sea, and air in the United States. According to the US Department of Transportation, it is projected that by 2020, trucks will carry the bulk of this freight (78.1 percent), followed by trains (14.6 percent), ships (7.1 percent), and planes (less than 1 percent).[8]

Tourism bolsters the US economy by $153 billion a year. Many Americans contribute to this economic force by spending their vacations at tourist sites within the country. Approximately 60 million visitors from other parts of the world also tour the United States each year.[9]

The United States has a large manufacturing sector—the largest in the world. Twenty-one percent of global manufactured products are made in the United States. That adds up to $1.7 trillion in goods being produced in the United States every year.[10] Beverages, food products, petroleum, furniture, and chemicals create big profits.

US CURRENCY

The US Currency is the dollar. The dollar is further broken down into cents. One dollar equals 100 cents. Dollars come in several denominations, ranging from $1 to $100. The front of each bill features a prominent American. These include:

$1: George Washington, the first US president

$2: Thomas Jefferson, the third US president

$5: Abraham Lincoln, the sixteenth US president

$10: Alexander Hamilton, the first secretary of the Treasury

$20: Andrew Jackson, the seventh US president

$50: Ulysses S. Grant, the eighteenth US president

$100: Benjamin Franklin, a US statesman

The flip side of US currency features various designs and motifs, depending on the bill. The bills are green in color and rectangular, measuring six and one-eighth by two and five-eighths inches (15.5 by 6.5 cm). Each bill has a unique serial number.

Coins issued in the US monetary system include the penny (one cent), the nickel (five cents), the dime (ten cents), the quarter (twenty-five cents), the half-dollar (fifty cents), and the dollar ($1).

But there has been a big drop-off in manufacturing over the past several decades. Cheaper labor in China and other parts of Asia have made these countries more attractive sources for this kind of production. Many simpler manufacturing jobs, such as textile manufacturing, are now outsourced overseas. More technical manufacturing jobs, such as those in aerospace equipment, aircraft, automobiles, and oil refining, have stayed in the United States. But efforts to cut costs have also affected jobs in this sector of manufacturing.

US currency

ENERGY

Due to a large industrial output, the United States uses 25 percent of the world's oil.[11] That total also includes using oil as fuel for transportation, for home and business heating, and as a source of electric power.

The United States produces approximately 2 billion barrels of crude oil a year.[12] But it has to import a little more than twice that much to meet its needs.[13] That makes the country vulnerable to disruptions in oil production abroad, especially in the volatile Middle East.

GROSS DOMESTIC PRODUCT

A country's economic performance is measured on an international scale called the gross domestic product (GDP). The GDP is the combined value of goods and services produced within a nation in a single year. The United States has an annual GDP of approximately $15 trillion, the largest in the world. The GDP of the United States represents approximately one-fifth of the world's GDP.[14]

In October 1973, oil-producing nations in the Middle East increased the price of oil and decreased production. That drove up prices, causing an oil crisis in the United States that forced the nation to rethink its energy policy. At first, other fossil fuels, such as coal and natural gas—both plentiful resources in the United States—were most heavily considered, and conservation was encouraged. Significant concerns over pollution and greenhouse gases from burning fossil fuels for energy have risen in recent years, however. Looking for a solution to curb the polluting emissions from fossil fuels and wean the nation from its dependence on foreign oil has prompted US leaders to start considering alternative energy sources. Among these sources are wind power, solar power, hydroelectric power, and geothermal energy.

TRADE

As the world's leading consumer of products, the United States is the top customer of most international companies. The nation's main trading

Legend:
- Aerospace
- Car Manufacture
- Chemicals
- Corn
- Cotton
- Food Processing
- Fruit
- Oil and Gas
- Research & Development
- Textiles
- Tourism
- Wheat

Resources of the United States

partners include Canada, China, the European Union, Mexico, and Japan. The United States is the world leader in imports. Motor vehicles, food, beverages, fuel, steel, and consumer goods are just a few of the products brought into the country. Aircraft and related parts, machinery, food, animal feed, beverages, and consumer products are shipped out of the country and around the world. Financial, insurance, technological, and other goods and services are also exported and imported.

The United States imports more than it exports, causing a trade deficit. That means the United States owes money to other nations for some of the products and services it imports. The nation's trading partners are willing to extend credit to the United States, but the US incurs debt as a result, which can weaken the overall economy.

ECONOMIC PROBLEMS

The shift in manufacturing overseas has led to high unemployment in the United States. Meanwhile, the technology industry has soared in certain parts of the United States, especially on the West Coast, but that often requires different skill sets than manufacturing. Workers who have been employed in manufacturing cannot easily make a transition to technology jobs. And the service industry has not been able to absorb all those who have lost their jobs in manufacturing. This loss of manufacturing

A man walks past graffiti calling out for and condemning lack of assistance in a poor part of Detroit, Michigan.

jobs, along with overall corporate downsizing and a sharp reduction in construction and government jobs, has hit the economy hard.

National unemployment in recent years has hovered in the 9 percent range. In 2012, areas of the job market showed signs of a mild recovery, reducing overall national unemployment to around 8 percent.[15] But in some job sectors, such as manufacturing, unemployment has remained high. Many people who lost full-time jobs have only been able to find part-time work to replace it. Some have not been able to find new jobs at all and have given up looking for work. They are referred to as "discouraged workers." When part-time workers who want full-time jobs and discouraged workers are added to the overall jobless rate, the unemployment rate in the United States reaches nearly 15 percent.[16] Another major problem in the US economy is the widening gap between the wealthiest citizens and the poorest. Over the past three decades, those at the

WOMEN IN THE WORKFORCE

There are more women in the workforce in the United States today than ever before. Women now make up almost half the labor force. In the 1940s only 30 percent of those employed in the country were women. Women currently hold approximately 50 percent of middle-management jobs. Women are also finding more jobs in some of the fastest-growing sectors of the economy, such as health care and retail sales. On the downside, some of these jobs are low paying and offer few benefits.[17]

lower end of the pay scale—20 percent of the workforce—have seen little or no increase in their salaries.[18] Meanwhile, the wealthiest 1 percent of the population have seen their wages triple over the past 30 years.[19] Overall, the average annual per-household income is $50,200.[20]

Approximately 155 million people have jobs in the United States.

CHAPTER 9

THE UNITED STATES TODAY

Life in the United States today varies as greatly as the people who live there. From north to south, by state and region, and down to neighborhoods and households, US citizens have diverse lives. Events, hobbies, holidays, and jobs are influenced by the sweeping changes in landscape and weather and by the wide range of cultures that make up the nation.

SECURITY

Although daily life varies greatly for many people, there are certain things that affect them all. Since the 9/11 terrorist attacks in 2001, the United States has felt less secure to many citizens. In a country that prides itself on freedom and privacy, people are now willing to make compromises in the name of security. Allowing pat-down searches at airports, passing through metal detectors in government buildings, permitting bags to

People's lives and families in the United States are as diverse as the nation's cultures and cities.

117

be searched, and carrying photo ID are all part of a new normal in an attempt to thwart terrorist attacks.

School shootings have also made headlines. One of the most notable took place in the small, quiet town of Littleton, Colorado, in 1999. The community was completely taken by surprise when two students at Columbine High School entered the school and shot and killed 12 other students and one teacher. An additional 24 people were injured before the two armed students killed themselves.

In addition to the Columbine shootings, other school killing sprees, including a shooting rampage at Virginia Tech in 2007, and a massacre in an Aurora, Colorado, movie theater in 2012, sparked debate over gun control in the United States. The right to bear arms is protected by the Second Amendment of the US Constitution, but it is also the government's role to provide for the well-being of its citizens by making an effort to protect them from random violence. Debate on these issues continues today.

PRIVACY

Some privacy has been sacrificed in the name of national security, but some has been voluntarily given up as part of the Information Age. Previous US generations were typically reluctant to give out any

Being scanned and patted down and having personal belongings searched has become a part of entering places such as stadiums and airports.

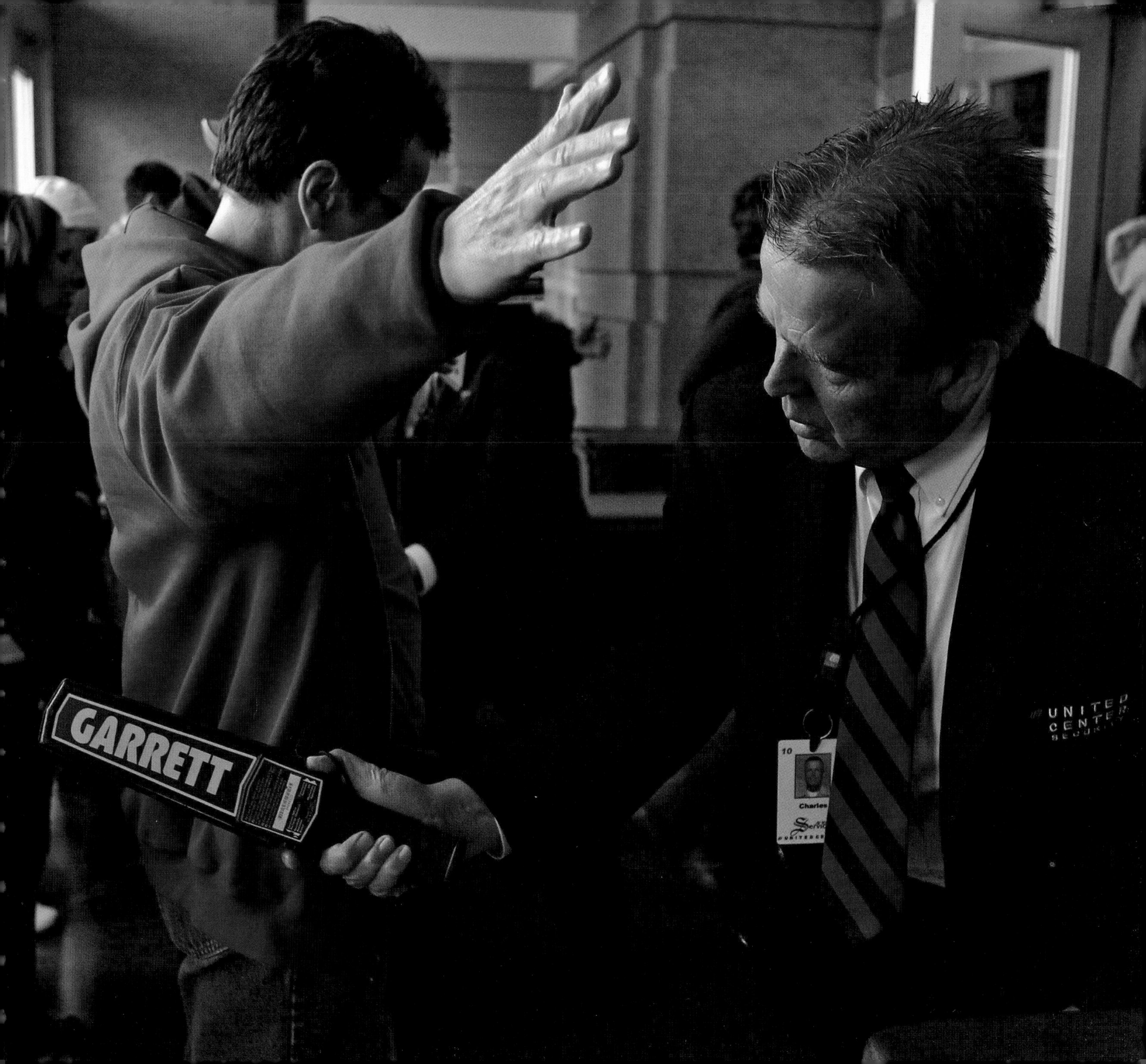
GARRETT
UNITED
Charles

information about themselves and were particularly unhappy about the government having access to it. The Internet and social networking Web sites such as Facebook, Twitter, and MySpace have changed that way of thinking. Now people commonly reveal private information about themselves that they would have once shared only with close friends. They do this on social networking Web sites that are not always secure and where many people can access it.

This has created a dilemma unique to today's citizens. People today wonder how much information is too much to reveal. They must consider how much information puts college acceptance, jobs, and personal relationships at risk or leaves them vulnerable to identity theft.

AFFORDING THE AMERICAN LIFESTYLE

The Information Age has presented other complexities as well. People in the United States live at vastly different economic levels, but in order to compete in academics or careers, keeping up with technology is a must for everyone. Most people are expected to have a computer, Internet access, and mobile phones for social reasons as well as for academic and work life. Besides having to pay the bills for mainstays of the American way of life—housing, clothing, food, and transportation—these new technological demands eat into the average American family's budget. Internet service, cell phones, computers, cable television, and other products and services often seem a necessity so as not to fall behind in the high-tech nation. But these technologies can be a struggle to afford even on average incomes.

The poverty rate in the United States is now the highest it has been in 20 years, at 46 million people, or 15 percent of the population.[1] More than 16.4 million children live in poverty in the United States, which is the richest country in the world.[2] For some segments of the population, the number of poor people is much higher. The poverty rate for African

Even better-off schools can suffer teacher layoffs, meaning fewer teachers for more students, who must then rely more heavily on technology than interaction.

Americans, for instance, is 10 percent higher than the national average, a legacy of racial discrimination in both education and the workplace.[3] Not everyone who lives in poverty is unemployed. Many poor Americans have jobs, but their salaries are so low they still fall below the poverty line. These individuals are considered the "working poor." Many income-strapped Americans also live in poorer neighborhoods where schools are not well equipped and educational opportunities for their children are limited. These families may not own personal computers and other electronic devices, and that puts children in these families at a disadvantage when it comes to future employment.

EDUCATION

Schooling is required in the United States. Children must begin school when they are approximately five years old and continue until they reach 16 to 18 years of age, depending on the state. A majority attend public school, but state-certified private and parochial schools are also options, as is homeschooling. Public schooling began in the 1840s, and Massachusetts was the first state to enact a compulsory school law, in 1852. It was not until 1918 that all 48 of the states in the union at that time adopted compulsory education laws.

Most children attend public school from kindergarten through twelfth grade. These schools are funded by federal, state, and local tax dollars. Local school boards set their own curricula and budgets with input from the state.

Both poorer school districts and those better off are facing a financial crisis in the United States today. As governments on all levels struggle to cut spending in response to lower revenues, less financial aid is being given to school districts. That often means cutting back on teachers, educational programs, after-school activities, and school equipment. It also translates into bigger class sizes, meaning each child gets less individualized attention.

The impact of these cuts to education differs in various regions of the country. In urban areas, where more people tend to live and schools have larger student populations, increased class sizes may leave practically no time for one-on-one student-teacher instruction time. In rural areas, cutting costs may mean keeping outdated computer equipment for many years. Regardless, the government budget crunch is squeezing the nation's educational system.

Any cuts to education are alarming. As of 2003, one out of every seven adults in the United States was illiterate, meaning they lacked the basic skills to read a newspaper or even the directions on a bottle of medication.[4] Illiteracy has a direct impact on job opportunities and how much money a person can earn. It also can be passed down from generation to generation because those who cannot read may not encourage their children to learn how to read either.

Education can fall victim not only to dwindling government budgets but to cash-strapped personal budgets as well. For example, the cost of getting a college

HIGHER EDUCATION

Despite rising costs, students continue to flock to US colleges and universities. A record 19.7 million students were enrolled in higher education in the fall of 2011. Females made up the majority of the students, with 11.2 million attending class. There were 8.5 million male students on campus. Of the 19.7 million students, 7.2 million were attending two-year colleges. With 3.2 million more students graduating from high school in 2012, the number of students attending college is likely to grow.[5]

education is soaring in the United States. The Great Recession, which began in 2008, took an enormous toll on the US economy and personally affected many people. In addition to rising product prices, jobs have been lost, homes have been repossessed, and the American way of life, which for many included the prospect of college, has been threatened. College tuition is climbing three times as fast as inflation. Even without this massive increase, today's students are facing a mountain of debt after graduating from college.

THE GREAT RECESSION

The economic decline referred to as the Great Recession was actually a global financial event. Some countries were hit harder than others. The fiscal downturn sent shock waves through the US economy. It caused a severe drop in consumer confidence, devalued homes, drove up the national debt, increased both personal and business bankruptcies, and dramatically increased the overall cost of living. Economists believe the Great Recession is over, but many Americans claim they are still feeling the pinch.

In addition, jobs are difficult to find for new college graduates. That is forcing these new members of the workforce to take jobs that pay less than they expected, only increasing the problem of looming college debt.

CUTBACKS IN BENEFITS

As the United States struggles to reshape its economy in the wake of the Great Recession, worker benefits are entering a new era. New workers face cutbacks in pensions and health benefits. Since World War II, most Americans traditionally received their health insurance through the workplace. Yet, in recent years, rapidly growing health-care costs have led many companies to cut back on health benefits or eliminate them altogether. This puts the burden of paying for health care on the individual. Although advancements have been made in controlling or eliminating many types of diseases, those advancements come at a steep cost that is often unattainable without health benefits. This has the most adverse effect on low- to middle-income wage earners. Approximately 44 million people in the United States have no health insurance, and another 38 million have inadequate health insurance.[6] The federal government is working to address the problem, but there is no guarantee proposed solutions will curb escalating health-care costs.

Although the United States faces challenges today, it has historically far exceeded expectations in facing adverse situations. Americans as a whole possess a strong resolve to overcome roadblocks standing in their way and approach challenges with optimism. The United States still leads the world in many economic areas, and the nation's economy is resilient. Much of the world looks to the United States for leadership. Entrepreneurship is alive and well. The United States remains a place where dreams can come true. As a nation of problem solvers, success is always only one great idea away.

Despite struggles and adversity, the American people continue to be a resilient society with a sense of unity.